How to Establish Credit in the U.S.

7 Proven Steps to Build Credit and Qualify for a Home, Car, Credit Cards & Business Loans in 90 Days

By Joe Correa

Published by Live Stronger Faster

This book is for educational and informational purposes only. The author and publisher are not engaged in rendering legal, financial, or other professional advice. Readers should consult a qualified professional before making any financial decisions.

First Edition

TABLE OF CONTENTS

Introduction.......... 4
Chapter 1: Understanding The U.S. Credit System.......... 12
Chapter 2: Building Credit From Scratch.......... 24
Chapter 3: Improving Your Credit Score.......... 37
Chapter 4: Financing Major Purchases.......... 51
Chapter 5: Avoiding Common Credit Pitfalls.......... 67
Chapter 6: Long-Term Credit Strategies.......... 76
Chapter 7: Turning Credit Into Capital, The Power Of Financial Leverage.......... 85
Conclusion.......... 98

INTRODUCTION

Hello, and welcome to *How to Establish Credit in the U.S.: 7 Proven Steps to Build Credit and Qualify for a Home, Car, Credit Cards & Business Loans in 90 Days.*

My name is **Joe Correa**, and I'm honored to be your guide on this powerful journey toward financial independence and long-term success.

Whether you're brand new to the United States, have lived here for years without credit, or recently discovered how critical a credit score is for your future, this book was designed with **you** in mind. I created this resource because I know exactly how confusing and overwhelming the U.S. credit system can be, especially when you're starting from zero.

In fact, I've personally worked with thousands of immigrants, international students, and first-time credit users who've faced this same challenge. They arrived in this country full of dreams and potential, only to be told "no" when applying for a car loan, a home mortgage, or even a simple credit card. Not because they had bad credit, **but because they had no credit at all.**

Let's be clear: having no credit history is not the same as having bad credit, but to the U.S. financial system, both are treated the same. That means doors are closed to you unless you know how to strategically open them. That's why this book exists, to give you the key.

Why Credit Matters More Than Ever

In today's world, credit affects almost everything:

- Renting an apartment
- Buying a car
- Getting approved for a mortgage
- Starting a business
- Qualifying for a cellphone plan
- Landing certain jobs
- Even how much you pay for car insurance

Credit isn't just a score, it's **a signal of trustworthiness**, a passport to opportunity. If you don't have it, you'll constantly run into barriers. But if you do have it, and you use it wisely, you can unlock doors that were previously out of reach.

Unfortunately, most immigrants and newcomers aren't taught how to build credit the right way. They're often given misinformation, denied repeatedly, or fall into traps that damage their score before they even begin.

That ends today.

Why I Created This book

My goal with this book is simple: **to teach you a clear, proven process for building credit, even if you have no Social Security number, no credit history, and no co-signer.**

You'll learn:

- The 7 exact steps I've used with clients to build strong credit in as little as 90 days
- How to get approved for your first credit account, even if you've been denied before
- What to avoid so you don't accidentally ruin your credit score
- How to qualify for a car loan, mortgage, or credit card without falling into debt
- And how to turn your credit into a tool for long-term financial freedom

I created this system based on real-world results, not theory. I've worked with everyday people, immigrants, students, single moms, freelancers, who followed these steps and went from **zero credit to homeownership** in under a year.

What Makes This Book Different?

Unlike many financial resources that use complicated jargon or assume you already know the basics, this book was created specifically for **people with no credit, limited experience, or language barriers.** I've simplified everything into easy-to-follow actions, real-life examples, and a system that works, even if English is not your first language or you've never taken a finance course in your life.

I've also included downloadable templates, checklists, and a 90-day plan you can follow step-by-step. You'll get clear answers to questions like:

- What's the difference between a secured and unsecured credit card?
- How long does it take to build a credit score?

- What are the safest ways to get approved without a co-signer?
- How many accounts should I open?
- Should I use credit to finance a business?

You'll find all of that, and more, inside.

Let's Get Personal

Let me tell you something important: **you don't have to be rich to build great credit. You don't need a perfect score to qualify for a home.** And you definitely don't need to feel stuck or embarrassed because you're starting from nothing.

I know this from personal experience.

When I started helping clients years ago, I realized that most financial success doesn't come from how much money you have, it comes from **how you manage what you have.** One of the biggest advantages you can create for yourself is a strong credit profile. It's a multiplier. It lowers the cost of borrowing. It increases your options. And most importantly, it gives you control.

You're not here to just survive in the U.S., you're here to thrive.

What to Expect

This book is divided into clear, actionable chapters. Each one focuses on a specific part of the credit-building process, from understanding the credit system to choosing the right first accounts, improving your score, and finally, using credit as a tool to fund major life goals like owning a home or starting a business.

At the end of each chapter, you'll find a real-life story to help illustrate the principles and make it easier to remember.

By the end of this book, you'll not only know how to build credit, you'll have the **confidence** and **plan** to do it the right way, without stress or confusion.

You've already taken the first step by pressing play. Now let's take the next step together.

This journey could change your life, not just today, but for generations to come. So whether you're listening on your commute, during a walk, or while working around the house, I want you to know this:

You belong here.

You're capable.

And your future just got a lot brighter.

Let's get started.

CHAPTER 1: UNDERSTANDING THE U.S. CREDIT SYSTEM

Before we talk about building credit, qualifying for loans, or getting approved for a home, car, or business funding, we need to take a step back and understand what credit actually is, and why it plays such a critical role in the U.S.

If you were raised in a different country, chances are credit didn't work the same way there. In fact, many cultures rely more heavily on cash or relationships with local banks rather than a formal credit scoring system. That's why the U.S. system can seem unfamiliar or even intimidating at first. But once you understand how it works, you'll realize that it's not about having money, it's about how you manage responsibility.

So let's start with the basics.

What Is Credit, and Why Does It Matter?

In simple terms, **credit is your ability to borrow money, and your history of repaying it.** When you use credit in the U.S., such as a credit card or a loan, your activity is recorded, tracked, and used to determine your financial reliability.

Here's why it matters:
Credit affects more than just borrowing. It affects whether you can rent an apartment, get approved for a phone plan, qualify for a mortgage, or even get certain jobs. Many employers, landlords, and lenders will check your credit to assess your trustworthiness. If you've never used credit, or if you've misused it, it can limit your options significantly.

But here's the good news:
Unlike income or immigration status, credit is something you can **build and control over time.** Even if you're starting from zero, you can create a strong credit profile by taking the right steps consistently.

What Is a Credit Report?

A **credit report** is a detailed history of how you've handled credit. It includes accounts you've opened, how much you've borrowed, your payment history, credit limits, any collections or late payments, and more.

There are three major credit bureaus in the United States:

- **Experian**
- **Equifax**
- **TransUnion**

These are independent companies that collect and store your credit information. Lenders, banks, and even utility companies report your financial activity to them. Then, the bureaus compile this data into your credit reports.

Each bureau may have slightly different data depending on which lenders report to them, so it's important to check all three. You are entitled to one free report per bureau per year, which you can get from AnnualCreditReport.com. This is the official site authorized by the U.S. government.

When reviewing your report, you should look for:

- Incorrect account balances
- Accounts you don't recognize

- Outdated information

- Misspelled names or wrong addresses

If something looks off, you can file a dispute to correct it. Fixing errors can significantly boost your credit score.

What Is a Credit Score?

Now let's talk about your **credit score**, a three-digit number that summarizes your credit history into a single, simple number. It usually ranges between **300 and 850**.

The higher your score, the more likely lenders are to trust you, and the better your financial opportunities become. With a high credit score, you can qualify for lower interest rates, bigger credit limits, and better terms when buying a home or car.

Your credit score is calculated using five main factors:

1. **Payment History – 35%**
   This is the most important factor. Do you pay your bills on time? One missed payment can drop your score

dramatically.

2. **Credit Utilization – 30%**
   This measures how much of your available credit you're using. Ideally, keep it below 30%. For example, if you have a $1,000 credit limit, try to keep your balance under $300.

3. **Length of Credit History – 15%**
   The longer your accounts have been open, the better. This is why starting early, even with small accounts, can benefit you later.

4. **Credit Mix – 10%**
   Lenders like to see that you can handle different types of credit, like credit cards, car loans, and student loans.

5. **New Credit – 10%**
   Opening too many new accounts at once can hurt your score, as it may signal financial instability.

Together, these five components paint a picture of how you manage credit. Understanding them helps you know exactly where to focus your efforts.

How to Check Your Score and Reports

Many people are afraid to check their credit, but checking your own score does **not** hurt your credit. In fact, reviewing your reports regularly is one of the smartest habits you can build.

Start by getting your free credit reports from **AnnualCreditReport.com**. Then, use free apps like **Credit Karma** or **Experian** to monitor your scores month to month. These apps also alert you to any suspicious activity, an important layer of protection.

If you find errors on your report, you can dispute them with each bureau directly. They are required by law to investigate and respond within 30 days. Correcting even one mistake, like a late payment that wasn't yours, can increase your score significantly.

Why This Knowledge Empowers You

When you understand how credit works, you're no longer vulnerable to misinformation, bad advice, or shady financial practices. You gain the confidence to apply for the right accounts, avoid predatory loans, and qualify for what you need.

Remember: credit isn't just about numbers, it's about access. Access to opportunities. To freedom. To the future you came here to build.

In the next chapter, we'll explore how to **start building credit from scratch**, even if you don't have a Social Security Number yet or have been denied credit before. This is where the journey really begins.

Let's take that next step together.

Ana's First Lesson in American Credit

Ana stepped off the plane at Miami International Airport with two suitcases and a heart full of hope. After 12 years of teaching literature in Bogotá, she had finally made the move to the United States to start a new life near her cousin Camila.

Her plan was clear: find a job, rent a small apartment, and slowly rebuild her life in this foreign but promising land.

By the second week, Ana had applied for a modest apartment in Little Havana. The landlord smiled politely as she handed over her paperwork, but an hour later, Ana received a text: "Application denied due to no credit history." She was stunned. She hadn't expected to get everything on the first try, but what did "no credit history" even mean?

The same thing happened when she tried to finance a used car. And again when she attempted to get a phone plan. "You need to build credit," said the sales associate, handing her a brochure she couldn't make sense of.

Ana had been financially responsible her whole adult life. She always paid bills on time, never borrowed more than she could afford, and managed her money carefully. But here, none of that mattered. In the eyes of American banks and businesses, Ana was invisible.

One Sunday, over coffee with her cousin Camila, Ana poured out her frustration. "I feel like I'm starting from zero, worse than zero. Back home, I had a reputation. Here, I can't even rent an apartment."

Camila nodded sympathetically. "That's because, here in the U.S., your financial trust is measured by something called a credit score. It's not about how much money you have, it's about how well you've handled credit in the past."

Ana leaned forward, eager to understand. "But I've never missed a payment in my life!"

"Yes, but they don't know that. You have to show them here," Camila replied. She pulled out her laptop and walked Ana through the basics.

She explained that credit in the U.S. is built through borrowing and repayment activity, which is tracked by three main credit bureaus, Equifax, Experian, and TransUnion. These companies collect data from banks, lenders, and even landlords. That data is used to generate a credit report and score.

Camila showed Ana how her credit score was calculated: 35% payment history, 30% credit utilization, 15% length of credit history, 10% credit mix, and 10% new credit inquiries. "Think of it like your financial GPA," she said.

Ana's head swirled. "So, I have to borrow money just to prove I can be trusted with money?" "Exactly," Camila laughed.

"Sounds backwards, but it works. Once you understand it, you can use it to your advantage."

They visited AnnualCreditReport.com, where Camila showed Ana how to pull her first free credit report. As expected, it was blank. No accounts, no history, no score.

But something shifted for Ana. Where there had been frustration and confusion, there was now a spark of determination. "If this is how the system works," she said, "then I'll learn the system."

The next day, Ana went to a local credit union and asked about secured credit cards. With Camila's help, she opened one using a $300 deposit. "Only use it for what you can pay off in full," Camila reminded her. Ana nodded. "Groceries only."

She also began keeping a notebook where she tracked every payment and due date. She wasn't just spending, she was building. She even downloaded a credit tracking app that let her check her score for free each month.

At her new job as a bilingual teaching assistant, Ana struck up a friendship with a fellow immigrant from Venezuela named Lucia. Over lunch one afternoon, Ana shared what she was learning about the credit system. Lucia confessed she had never applied for credit either, fearing rejection. Inspired, she asked Ana to help her get started.

Three months later, Ana saw her first credit score: 687. It wasn't perfect, but it was hers. She had created it. That same week, she was approved for a basic cell phone plan. By month five, she qualified for an apartment rental on her own, no co-signer needed.

Ana didn't stop there. She read articles on credit-building, signed up for a financial literacy workshop, and even joined a Facebook group for immigrants navigating the U.S. financial system. She started mentoring others who were in the same shoes she had worn just months earlier.

What Ana learned most was that credit wasn't just about getting approved, it was about access. Access to choices. Access to fair rates. Access to independence. It wasn't personal, it was math, logic, behavior, and timing.

One day, after helping Lucia pull her first report, Ana looked back at the blank credit report she had seen months ago. "Back then, I felt like I didn't exist here," she said. "But now I know, I just had to speak the financial language."

She smiled as she thought about her old students in Bogotá. If they could see her now, learning a brand new system in a brand new land, they'd be proud. And she was proud of herself. Ana didn't just learn credit, she mastered it. And with every on-time payment, every smart decision, she was writing a new story, one of resilience, empowerment, and hope.

CHAPTER 2: BUILDING CREDIT FROM SCRATCH

Now that you understand how the U.S. credit system works, it’s time to roll up your sleeves and take action. If you're starting with no credit history at all, this chapter is for you.

The most important thing I want you to remember is this: **you are not behind.**

You are simply at the beginning, and beginnings are powerful.

Many people think that credit is something that just “happens” over time. But in reality, **you can begin building strong credit right now**, even if you’ve never borrowed money, don’t have a credit score, or have recently moved to the U.S. with no financial history.

So let’s break it down and give you a clear path to follow.

Step 1: Open Your First Secured Credit Card

A secured credit card is often the best starting point. Why? Because it's one of the easiest types of credit to get approved for, even if you have no credit history at all.

Here's how it works:

You provide a refundable security deposit, typically between $200 and $500. That amount becomes your credit limit. For example, if you deposit $300, your limit is $300. You can use the card just like any other credit card, for groceries, gas, small purchases, or monthly bills.

What matters most is **how you manage it**. Use the card for basic purchases, then **pay off the full balance every month, on time.** This shows lenders you are responsible and trustworthy. After 6–12 months of on-time payments, many banks will upgrade your card to an unsecured one and return your deposit.

If you're not sure where to get a secured card, look for major banks like **Capital One, Discover, or your local credit union.** Many offer beginner-friendly options with no annual fee and credit reporting to all three bureaus.

Step 2: Become an Authorized User

This strategy is often overlooked but can be incredibly powerful, especially if you have a trusted family member or friend with good credit.

Ask them to add you as an **authorized user** on one of their existing credit cards. When they do, their positive credit history, such as account age and on-time payments, may start appearing on your credit report too. You don't even need to use the card yourself.

This can dramatically improve your credit score in a short period of time, assuming the account has low utilization and no late payments. Just make sure to talk openly with the cardholder so they understand how it works and are comfortable with the responsibility.

Note: Not all credit card companies report authorized users to all three bureaus, so confirm this before proceeding.

Step 3: Take Out a Credit-Builder Loan

Next, consider applying for a **credit-builder loan**. These are small loans, often between $300 and $1,000, designed specifically for people who are new to credit.

Here's how they work:

The money is not given to you upfront. Instead, it's placed in a locked savings account while you make monthly payments. Once the loan is fully repaid, the money is released to you.

So what's the benefit? **Your on-time payments are reported to the credit bureaus.** That means even if you didn't technically "spend" the loan, you're building credit each month by showing consistent repayment behavior.

You can find credit-builder loans through local credit unions, online banks like **Self** or **Kikoff**, or community development financial institutions (CDFIs). They're low-risk, low-interest, and highly effective.

Step 4: Make Payments On Time, Every Time

No matter which tool you use, a secured card, credit-builder loan, or authorized user account, **the number one rule is to pay on time. Every time.**

Why? Because **payment history makes up 35% of your credit score**. Even a single late payment can drop your score by 50 to 100 points, and that's a big setback when you're just getting started.

Set up auto-pay or payment reminders so you never miss a due date. And always pay at least the minimum, though paying the full balance is even better.

Building credit is like building trust: it takes time, but one mistake can undo a lot of progress. Stay consistent and treat every payment as a chance to prove your reliability.

Step 5: Keep Your Credit Utilization Low

Your **credit utilization** is the percentage of your credit limit that you're using at any given time. Let's say your secured credit card has a $300 limit. If you spend $270 each month, your utilization is 90%, and that's considered too high.

To keep your score healthy, aim to use **no more than 30%** of your available limit. Even better? Stay under 10% if you can. So if your limit is $300, try to keep your balance under $90. Pay it off in full each month to avoid interest and show lenders you're in control.

This one habit alone can have a huge positive effect on your credit score.

Step 6: Track Your Progress

Once you start building credit, it's important to **monitor your progress.** This keeps you motivated and lets you catch errors or fraud early.

You can use free tools like:

- **Credit Karma**
- **Credit Sesame**
- **Experian app**

- Or your bank's credit monitoring feature

These platforms let you check your score, see changes over time, and understand how your actions affect your credit. Watching your score go up, even slowly, can be incredibly motivating.

You're Building a Foundation

Building credit from scratch is like planting a tree. You don't see the full results immediately, but each step adds up.

Open your first account. Use it wisely. Make on-time payments. Keep your balances low. Track your progress.

In just 90 days, you'll likely start seeing meaningful changes. And over time, your responsible behavior will open doors to larger credit limits, lower interest rates, and opportunities you never had access to before.

In the next chapter, we'll go deeper into how to **improve your credit score** even faster, by correcting errors, increasing limits, and mastering the five factors that drive your score. Let's keep building.

Samir's Path from No Score to Strong Score

Samir stepped onto the balcony of his new apartment in Austin, Texas, sipping his morning chai. He had earned his master's degree in computer science just three months earlier and landed a job at a promising tech startup. Everything was falling into place, except for one frustrating reality.

He still didn't have a credit score.

Despite earning a respectable salary and being responsible with money, Samir quickly learned that having no credit was just as limiting as having bad credit. He found out the hard way when he applied to rent a car for a weekend trip to San Antonio. "Sorry," the agent told him. "You need a credit history for that." Even when he tried to sign up for a monthly gym membership, the company ran a credit check. Rejected again.

Samir was stunned. "I have the money," he told his friend Neha over dinner. "I've never been in debt. Isn't that supposed to be a good thing?"

Neha smiled knowingly. “In India, yes. In the U.S., not really. Here, lenders want to see that you’ve borrowed money and paid it back responsibly. No history means no score, and no trust.”

It felt unfair. Samir had grown up with a culture of saving, avoiding debt, and paying in cash. Now, all that financial discipline seemed invisible in his new home.

But Samir wasn’t one to give up easily. He took Neha’s advice and started researching how to build credit from scratch. He quickly came across the concept of a secured credit card . It sounded strange at first, putting down a cash deposit just to borrow his own money, but he saw the logic. It was a foot in the door.

He applied for a secured card through his local credit union and was approved for a $300 limit. The bank held $300 of his own money as collateral. Samir made a promise to himself: he would use the card only for necessities, pay off the balance in full every month, and never carry debt.

The first thing he charged was a $42 internet bill. Then a tank of gas. He paid it off before the due date and kept going. He didn’t touch more than $90 a month, keeping his utilization below 30%, and always paid in full.

Two months later, Samir asked his cousin Rohan, who had been in the U.S. for five years, if he could add him as an authorized user to one of his long-standing credit cards.

"Sure," Rohan said. "I've had this card for six years and always paid it on time." Being added to Rohan's account meant Samir could benefit from the card's history, even though he wouldn't actually use it. It was like inheriting financial credibility.

Samir's next move was opening a credit-builder loan from a local online bank. The loan amount was only $500, but the funds were held in a secured account while Samir made monthly payments of $45. It felt a bit silly at first, paying a loan for money he couldn't access, but he realized it was about building a payment history. Each month, the bank reported his on-time payments to the credit bureaus.

Around the same time, Samir also made a budget. Not just for tracking spending, but to stay disciplined with credit. He created a spreadsheet where he tracked his card balances, due dates, payment confirmations, and current score estimates from apps like Credit Karma.

Three months later, Samir logged into his credit monitoring app and saw a score for the first time: 689.

He nearly dropped his phone. He called Neha right away.

“I have a score!” he said, laughing. “And it’s not terrible!”

“You built it, one responsible step at a time,” she replied. “Now keep it going.”

With his score established, Samir received his first pre-qualified credit card offer in the mail. It wasn’t flashy, but it had no annual fee and a $1,000 credit limit. He applied and was approved. This gave him more available credit, which helped lower his utilization rate even further.

He used the new card to pay for recurring expenses like Netflix, Spotify, and a few grocery runs, making sure everything was paid in full each month. His spreadsheet remained updated. If his balance ever climbed above $100, he paid it early, even before the statement closed.

Six months later, Samir had a credit score of 734. His financial behavior hadn’t changed much, he still lived simply, saved diligently, and avoided unnecessary purchases, but now the system recognized his efforts.

That fall, Samir decided to lease a car. The dealership finance officer reviewed his credit profile and nodded in approval.

"You're in the 700s," she said. "You'll get a great rate."

For Samir, it was a turning point. He was no longer invisible in the system. He had built credibility the American way, not by chance, but by strategy.

And he wasn't done yet. He subscribed to a credit tracking service and began setting new goals. First, he would get his score above 760. Then, he'd start building business credit for a side project he was planning. Eventually, he wanted to buy a condo, and now, he was on track.

But Samir wasn't just building credit for himself. He became the go-to person in his immigrant community for credit questions. He gave workshops at the local community center, wrote blog posts in Hindi and English, and even helped his older brother open a secured card when he moved to the U.S. six months later.

"Your score isn't about showing off," he often said. "It's about access, to homes, jobs, even opportunities you haven't thought of yet. Build it wisely, and it'll serve you for life."

Samir's journey from no score to strong score didn't happen overnight. But with patience, planning, and purpose, he turned a system that once shut him out into a tool that opened doors.

CHAPTER 3: IMPROVING YOUR CREDIT SCORE

If you've already started building credit or if you're working to repair a damaged score, this chapter is your next big step. Whether you're looking to raise your score by 20 points or 200, the strategies you'll learn here can help you make real, measurable progress.

Let's be clear, **your credit score isn't fixed or final**. It's dynamic. It changes based on your actions. That means no matter where you're starting from, whether you're at 520 or 720, there are always steps you can take to improve. And often, the biggest changes come from the smallest corrections, consistently applied over time.

Let's explore the most effective strategies to boost your credit score and unlock greater financial freedom.

1. Spot and Dispute Credit Report Errors

One of the fastest and easiest ways to raise your credit score is by removing inaccurate information.

You'd be surprised how often credit reports contain mistakes, everything from wrong account balances to duplicate accounts, or even loans that don't belong to you. These errors can drag your score down without you even knowing it.

That's why the first step is to **pull your credit reports from all three major bureaus:**

- **Experian**
- **Equifax**
- **TransUnion**

Visit AnnualCreditReport.com to access them for free. Go through each line carefully. Are there accounts you don't recognize? Balances that seem off? Late payments that you're sure you paid on time?

If you find anything suspicious, don't panic, **you have the right to dispute any inaccurate information.** Each bureau allows you to file a dispute online. By law, they must investigate and respond within 30 days.

In many cases, simply disputing a reporting error can lead to a boost of 50 to 100 points, almost instantly. It's one of the most overlooked tools in credit repair.

2. Lower Your Credit Utilization Ratio

After payment history, **credit utilization** is the second most important factor in your score, making up **30%** of your total. This refers to the percentage of your available credit that you're currently using.

Let's say you have a credit card with a $1,000 limit and you carry a $700 balance. Your utilization rate is 70%, and that's way too high in the eyes of lenders.

Ideally, you want to keep utilization below 30%. Even better? Below 10%.

Here's how to fix it:

- **Pay down high balances as aggressively as possible**

- **Spread your purchases across multiple cards if you have more than one**

- **Request a credit limit increase, but only if you're sure you won't be tempted to spend more**

For example, if you increase your limit from $1,000 to $2,000, that same $700 balance drops your utilization from 70% to just 35%, giving your score room to rise. Just remember, this is a strategy to reduce your ratio, not to increase your spending power.

3. Prioritize On-Time Payments

There's no sugarcoating it, **on-time payments are the single most important factor in your credit score**, accounting for **35%** of it.

Even one missed or late payment can stay on your credit report for **up to seven years**. That's why it's critical to build habits that make late payments nearly impossible.

Here's how:

- Set up **automatic payments** for at least the minimum amount due on each account
- Use **calendar reminders** or budgeting apps to track due dates
- If you're short on cash, **communicate with lenders early**, some may offer grace periods or hardship plans

Think of each on-time payment as a deposit into your future financial freedom. It builds trust with lenders and steadily improves your score month after month.

4. Avoid Unnecessary Hard Inquiries

It might feel tempting to apply for multiple credit cards or loans to try and boost your access to funds. But here's the catch, **each time you apply for credit, a hard inquiry is placed on your report.**

Too many hard inquiries in a short time period can signal desperation to lenders and **cause a temporary dip in your score.**

So be selective. Only apply for credit when:

- You have a high chance of approval
- You actually need it
- You're spacing out applications over time

Hard inquiries usually affect your score for 12 months and fall off your report after 24 months. Avoid applying for multiple accounts at once, especially if you're trying to raise your score quickly.

If you're comparing rates for a car loan or mortgage, try to do it within a 14–30 day window. Multiple inquiries for the same type of loan during this time are usually treated as one inquiry.

5. Build Strong Credit Habits That Stick

Improving your credit score is not a one-time fix, it's a lifestyle. And small habits make a big difference over time.

Here's how to build a credit-friendly life:

- **Keep your oldest accounts open** , they help with the length of your credit history
- **Mix it up** , maintain a healthy mix of revolving credit (like credit cards) and installment credit (like auto loans or credit-builder loans)
- **Use less than you can afford** , just because you're approved for a $5,000 limit doesn't mean you should spend it
- **Check your credit score monthly** , use apps like Credit Karma or Experian to track your progress
- **Set financial goals** , like increasing your score by 50 points in 6 months or qualifying for a mortgage in a year

Consistency is the secret. The longer you stay on track, the more your score reflects your stability.

Final Thoughts

Improving your credit score doesn't require perfection. What it requires is **awareness, discipline, and a strategy.**

Every on-time payment, every reduced balance, and every good habit pushes you forward. And as your score improves, so do your financial options, lower interest rates, higher approval chances, and greater flexibility to pursue your goals.

In the next chapter, we'll dive into how to **use your improved credit to finance major purchases**, like a car, a home, or even a business. This is where all your hard work starts to pay off in real ways.

Let's keep going, you're doing great.

Maya's Road to Recovery

Maya stood in line at the grocery store, holding a half-full basket and hoping her debit card wouldn't get declined again. At 29, she had a good job, a car, and a modest apartment in Queens, New York. But behind the scenes, her financial life was crumbling.

She wasn't new to credit. In fact, that was part of the problem.

At 21, Maya got her first credit card on her college campus. "Build your credit today!" the representative promised, handing her a free t-shirt and a folder. Maya didn't know much about interest rates or utilization, but she figured if she made the minimum payment, everything would be fine.

By the time she was 25, Maya had five credit cards. She never missed a payment, at first. But when her mom got sick back in El Salvador and Maya had to cover medical bills and travel expenses, the debt piled up fast. She maxed out two of her cards, fell behind on payments, and opened a new store card just to buy groceries.

Eventually, the late fees started to snowball. Calls from collections came daily. Maya felt overwhelmed and ashamed.

"I'm not irresponsible," she would tell herself. "I just didn't know better."

By the time she turned 28, her credit score had dropped to 520. She couldn't qualify for an apartment without a co-signer. Her auto loan had a 17% interest rate. Even her employer's finance department questioned her when she applied for a relocation benefit.

Maya knew something had to change. One night, she Googled, "How to fix my credit score." What she found surprised her. There were blogs, YouTube channels, free credit counseling services, even community classes. She signed up for a free credit workshop at a local nonprofit, and that workshop changed everything.

The instructor was a soft-spoken woman named Gloria, a former banker who now volunteered teaching financial literacy. Gloria explained how payment history made up 35% of Maya's credit score, and how utilization, credit age, inquiries, and credit mix filled out the rest.

"But most importantly," she said, "you need to know what's on your credit report. Pull it. Read it. Own it."

Maya left the class with a checklist and determination. That night, she went to AnnualCreditReport.com and requested her reports from all three credit bureaus.

What she found stunned her.

There were three collection accounts she didn't recognize. One was from a medical lab she'd never used. Another was an old phone bill she'd already paid but never disputed. There were also two late payments on a student loan she hadn't realized were reported 60 days late during her forbearance period.

The next day, Maya filed disputes on all three accounts. She uploaded bank statements, payment confirmations, and letters. Thirty days later, two of the items were removed, and her score jumped by 41 points.

Encouraged, Maya kept going. She made a spreadsheet with all her accounts: balances, minimum payments, interest rates, and due dates. She used color coding, green for current, yellow for nearing limit, red for delinquent.

Her first goal: catch up on all late accounts. She picked up extra shifts at work, sold some designer bags online, and used the money to pay off a $450 overdue card that had been collecting interest for months.

Then she focused on credit utilization . She had $3,200 in total available credit and was using more than $2,800, an 88% ratio. Her goal was to bring it down to below 30%, ideally under 10%.

She started by paying off her smallest balance, just $280 on a store card. Then she tackled her highest interest card, a gas card with a 27% APR. Slowly, she watched her balances drop and her score climb. She also set all her cards to automatic minimum payments , so she'd never miss a due date again. On top of that, she added calendar reminders on her phone to make additional payments mid-month to further lower her balances before the statement cut-off.

Maya didn't just work on paying things down. She also started building new, positive habits . She signed up for Experian Boost, which added her phone and utility payments to her credit report. It gave her a quick 18-point bump.

At her bank's suggestion, she asked for a credit limit increase on one of her oldest cards. To her surprise, they approved it, raising her limit from $1,000 to $2,500. That change alone dropped her utilization by 15%.

But Maya wasn't looking for quick fixes, she wanted real change. She began tracking her progress monthly. In a notebook, she wrote down her score, total debt, and payment dates. She celebrated small wins: when her score hit 600, when her total debt fell below $2,000, when a collection account aged past the statute of limitations.

By the time her 30th birthday arrived, Maya's credit score was 673.

She applied for a new apartment, no co-signer needed. She refinanced her auto loan and cut the interest rate in half. She even got approved for a travel rewards card, which she used only for groceries and gas, paying it off every week.

But perhaps the most meaningful change was emotional.

Maya no longer felt afraid to open mail or answer unknown calls. She no longer avoided looking at her bank account. She had gone from feeling ashamed to feeling empowered.

She started mentoring younger colleagues at her job, hosting lunchtime sessions on budgeting and credit. She even helped her cousin dispute an old medical bill that had been dragging down her score.

"Credit isn't about being perfect," Maya told them. "It's about being consistent, being aware, and making the system work for you."

Today, Maya's score hovers near 730. She checks her report every few months, keeps her utilization under 10%, and hasn't missed a payment in over two years.

But more than the number, Maya values the confidence she gained, the peace of mind, the sense of control, and the opportunity to create a future on her own terms.

CHAPTER 4: FINANCING MAJOR PURCHASES

This chapter is where credit starts to feel real, when it moves beyond theory and becomes a tool to help you achieve life-changing goals. Whether you're buying your first car, planning to purchase a home, or funding a business idea, your credit score plays a huge role in the outcome.

Used wisely, credit opens doors. Used carelessly, it can lead to overwhelming debt. The difference lies in understanding how financing works and being prepared before you apply. Let's walk through how to use credit responsibly to finance major purchases.

1. Financing a Car , What You Need to Know

For many, buying a car is the first major credit-based purchase they make. Whether you're purchasing a new vehicle or a reliable used one, it's a big financial commitment that requires thoughtful planning.

The first step? **Check your credit score.**

Your score directly affects the interest rate you'll be offered. A high score could save you thousands over the life of the loan, while a low score could cost you much more in interest.

Before heading to a dealership, get **pre-approved** through your bank or a credit union. Pre-approval gives you an idea of the loan amount, term length, and interest rate you qualify for, **without the pressure of a salesperson standing over you.** It also strengthens your position as a buyer.

Create a budget that goes beyond the car's price. Include:

- Sales tax
- Title and registration fees
- Insurance premiums
- Expected maintenance costs
- Fuel and ongoing operating expenses

When applying for the loan, lenders will review more than just your score, they'll look at:

- Your income
- Employment status
- Debt-to-income (DTI) ratio
- Any down payment you can provide

A down payment of 10–20% can reduce the loan amount and increase your approval chances. It also shows lenders that you're financially committed.

Remember: the best loan isn't always the one with the lowest monthly payment. Shorter terms typically have higher monthly payments but much less interest over time.

2. Buying a Home , From Dream to Reality

Owning a home is a common part of the American Dream, but it requires strategic preparation.

Before applying for a mortgage:

- Pull your credit reports and correct any errors
- Work to improve your score, especially if it's under 700
- Calculate how much home you can afford based on income and savings

A minimum credit score of 620 is often required for most mortgages. However, scores of **700 and above** typically unlock the best rates and the widest variety of loan programs.

Next, start saving for a down payment. While **FHA loans** allow as little as 3.5% down, putting down 10–20% can reduce your monthly payments and eliminate private mortgage insurance (PMI).

Here are some common loan types to consider:

- **Conventional Loans** – Best for buyers with strong credit and solid income
- **FHA Loans** – More lenient requirements, great for first-time buyers
- **VA Loans** – Available to eligible veterans, often require no down payment
- **USDA Loans** – For homes in rural areas, with low or no down payment

Shop around for mortgage lenders and get **pre-approved** before you start house hunting. Sellers take pre-approved buyers more seriously, and you'll have a clear picture of what you can afford.

Also, compare interest rates, fees, and repayment terms before choosing a lender. Don't forget closing costs, they typically add another **2%–5%** of the home's price.

A home loan is a long-term commitment, so educate yourself and surround yourself with professionals, agents, lenders, and credit advisors, who can guide you through the process.

3. Financing or Expanding a Business

If you're an entrepreneur or plan to start a business in the U.S., credit will become an essential funding tool.

Many startups begin by using **personal credit**, credit cards, personal loans, or home equity, to fund operations. This works temporarily, but separating your **business and personal finances** is key to long-term growth and protection.

Start by:

- Registering your business as an LLC or corporation
- Opening a business checking account
- Applying for an **Employer Identification Number (EIN)**

- Setting up a **business credit file** with Dun & Bradstreet

Once you've established business credit, you can apply for:

- **Business credit cards**
- **Lines of credit**
- **Term loans**
- **SBA (Small Business Administration) loans**

Before applying, prepare a solid **business plan** that outlines your goals, revenue projections, and how the funds will be used. Strong documentation builds confidence with lenders.

And remember: your **personal credit still matters.** Many lenders will review your personal credit score when you're just starting out.

Building both business and personal credit over time gives you more financing options, better terms, and greater credibility.

4. Know the Terms Before You Sign

No matter what you're financing, whether it's a vehicle, home, or business, **always read the fine print.**

Understand the key elements of any loan:

- **Interest rate (APR):** Is it fixed or variable? What is the total interest over the life of the loan?

- **Repayment term:** A shorter term may mean higher payments but less interest. A longer term lowers the payment but increases the total cost.

- **Monthly payment:** Can you afford it comfortably alongside your other obligations?

- **Fees:** Are there application fees, loan origination fees, late fees, or early payoff penalties?

- **Total loan cost:** How much will you end up paying in total by the time the loan is paid off?

Don't rely solely on the monthly payment, it can be misleading. For example, a $15,000 car loan over 5 years may seem manageable at $300/month, but over time you may end up paying **$18,000 or more** depending on the interest rate.

Ask questions. Get multiple offers. Compare all options.

This one step could save you thousands and keep your credit profile healthy.

Final Thoughts

Using credit to finance major purchases is not something to fear, it's a sign of financial progress and trustworthiness. But it must be done **strategically and with full awareness** of the responsibilities that come with debt.

Be proactive:

- Strengthen your credit before applying
- Know what lenders look for
- Understand every term of the agreement
- Only borrow what you can confidently repay

Let's keep moving forward.

David's Dream Car and First Home

David leaned back in the plastic chair at the car dealership in Houston, nervously flipping through a brochure for a 2020 Honda Civic. The salesman, all bright smiles and optimism, had just stepped away to "run the numbers." It was David's first time financing a vehicle, and while he felt proud, he also wasn't entirely sure what to expect.

Just two years earlier, David had paid cash for everything. Growing up in Lagos, Nigeria, his parents taught him that debt was dangerous and credit cards were a trap. "If you can't afford it in cash, don't buy it," his father used to say.

But that belief didn't translate well when David moved to the United States at 26 to work as a civil engineer. Here, building credit wasn't optional, it was essential. It started when he tried to lease an apartment downtown. Despite having $10,000 in savings and a steady paycheck, the landlord declined his application. "No credit history," they said.

That moment changed everything.

David began learning about the U.S. credit system. He opened a secured credit card with a $500 deposit and used it carefully, never spending more than $100 per month and always paying it in full. He became an authorized user on his cousin's long-standing card and later took out a small credit-builder loan from his local bank. Within six months, he had a score of 702.

Now, two years later, he was ready for his first major purchase: a car.

The salesman returned, waving a printout.

"Good news! With your credit score at 748 and stable income, we can offer 3.4% APR on a 60-month term. And no co-signer needed."

David exhaled. Relief and pride mixed in his chest. "Let's do it," he said.

The dealership processed the paperwork, and by that evening, David was behind the wheel of his first financed car. The monthly payment fit within his budget, and he even opted for additional gap coverage just to be safe.

But David didn't stop there. With the car successfully financed and his credit profile growing stronger, his sights shifted to an even bigger dream: homeownership.

He'd been renting a one-bedroom apartment near his office and paying $1,400 per month. It wasn't terrible, but he wanted stability. He wanted to invest in something permanent.

The first step was research. David dove into online articles, YouTube videos, and even visited local first-time homebuyer workshops. That's where he first learned about FHA loans, government-backed mortgages that allowed lower credit scores and down payments as low as 3.5%.

At the workshop, he met a mortgage broker named Sheila who offered to run some preliminary numbers for him.

"With your current credit score and employment history, you're a strong FHA candidate," she said. "But you'll need to show two years of consistent work and save for the down payment and closing costs."

David went home and mapped out a savings strategy. He cut unnecessary expenses, eating out, streaming services, and weekly game purchases. He opened a high-yield savings account and labeled it "House Fund." Every paycheck, he deposited $400 without fail.

Within nine months, he had saved $12,000, enough for a down payment, moving costs, and a cushion for emergencies.

The next step was getting pre-approved for a mortgage. David gathered his tax returns, W-2s, bank statements, pay stubs, and identification. Sheila submitted the application to several lenders and got him pre-approved for $270,000 with a 4.1% interest rate.

Pre-approval in hand, David started house hunting.

It was more emotional than he expected. The first house he saw smelled like mildew. The second was too far from work. The third had neighbors who blasted music all day. But the fourth, an older brick home with a renovated kitchen and fenced yard, felt right.

He made an offer below asking, and after a short negotiation, the seller agreed. The home inspection showed only minor issues. The appraisal came back clean.

Then came the final hurdle: closing.

David was bombarded with documents: loan disclosures, settlement statements, title insurance agreements. But he was ready. He had done his homework. He understood the mortgage terms: 30-year fixed, 4.1% APR, $1,335 monthly payment including taxes and insurance.

On closing day, David signed 42 pages and handed over a cashier's check for the down payment.

As the agent handed him the keys, David stood still for a moment.

He'd done it. He had used credit, wisely, patiently, strategically, to finance a car and a home. He had turned numbers and paperwork into real, tangible assets. The first night in his new home, he walked from room to room, still in disbelief. He cooked dinner in his own kitchen and ate at a folding table in the living room, surrounded by boxes. It was quiet. It was his.

Over the next few months, David automated his mortgage payments and set up alerts for due dates. He checked his credit report quarterly and kept his utilization low. His credit score continued to climb, reaching 765 by the end of the year.

He also started mentoring younger colleagues at his firm who were new to the U.S. "Start early," he'd tell them. "Don't wait until you need credit to begin building it."

He shared his story, how he had gone from no credit to owning a car and a home within three years. He explained how credit wasn't about debt, it was about leverage, responsibility, and long-term thinking.

David didn't stop there. He began reading about real estate investing. He took a weekend course on rental properties and even attended open houses for duplexes. His dream now included owning rental units, passive income that could support him in retirement.

But for now, he was content. He had achieved two milestones that once felt impossible.

And he did it not by chasing shortcuts or gaming the system, but by learning, planning, and applying what he'd learned one decision at a time.

David's story wasn't just about buying a car or a house.

It was about building a foundation.

And now that he had it, there was no limit to what he could build next.

In the next chapter, we'll shift gears and talk about **managing credit responsibly over time**, building the habits that protect your score, prevent debt, and ensure that your financial growth is sustainable.

CHAPTER 5: AVOIDING COMMON CREDIT PITFALLS

Many people unknowingly damage their credit. Let's talk about how to avoid the most common mistakes: - Missing payments and how to set up payment reminders - Carrying high balances and the impact on utilization - Applying for too much credit in a short time - Closing old accounts and how it affects your score - Ignoring your credit report and missing errors Missing payments is one of the most damaging credit mistakes. Even one late payment can drop your score significantly and stay on your report for years. Use reminders, calendar alerts, or automatic payments to ensure every bill is paid on time. Carrying high balances also harms your score. Try to keep your credit utilization below 30%, and if possible, below 10% for optimal results. Paying off high-interest cards first can help reduce debt faster and save money. Be cautious about applying for multiple credit cards or loans in a short period. Each application creates a hard inquiry, which can lower your score temporarily. Multiple inquiries may raise red flags with lenders. Closing old accounts may seem like a good way to simplify your finances, but it can actually shorten your credit history and increase your utilization. Unless a card has high fees or you're at risk of overspending, consider keeping old accounts open. Lastly, don't ignore your credit report. Review it regularly for errors or signs of fraud. Disputing inaccuracies quickly can prevent long-term damage. By avoiding these common mistakes, you can protect the credit foundation you've worked hard to build.

Lina's Lessons from Mistakes

Lina closed her salon early that Friday evening, flipping the "Open" sign to "Closed" and drawing down the security gate with a long sigh. The shop had been unusually quiet all week. Fewer clients meant fewer tips, and fewer tips meant trouble.

She walked to her car, a compact SUV with three missed payments, and sat in the driver's seat a few moments before turning the key. The dashboard lit up with a check engine light, again.

Lina was exhausted, not just from working on her feet all day, but from the stress that had crept into every part of her life. And at the center of it all was one thing: her credit.

She wasn't new to credit. In fact, she had built good credit when she first moved to New Jersey from the Dominican Republic. When she opened her salon six years ago, she had a credit score in the high 700s. She was approved for three business credit cards, financed salon equipment, and even helped her younger sister get her first auto loan.

But then came 2020.

The pandemic hit small businesses like a tsunami. Her salon, once buzzing with customers and chatter, was empty for months. She tried to pivot, offering at-home kits, Zoom consultations, even TikTok tutorials, but the income dried up. Rent was still due. Utilities piled up. Credit card bills went unpaid. “I’ll catch up next month,” she told herself. But next month turned into the next quarter, and before she knew it, her credit score dropped from 783 to 586.

She maxed out two of her cards and missed five payments. One account was sent to collections. Her salon lease renewal was denied due to her business credit, and she had to move locations, losing a chunk of loyal customers in the process.

By the time things began reopening, Lina was buried in debt, and her phone buzzed daily with creditor calls.

The worst part wasn’t the debt, it was the shame.

She stopped answering unknown numbers. She ignored mail. She even turned down a date because she didn’t want to explain why her credit card was declined.

One afternoon, while waiting at the DMV to renew her license, she overheard a woman talking about a free credit counseling workshop at the community center.

Lina jotted down the details and attended the following week.

The workshop was small, just eight people and a speaker named Rafael, a former loan officer turned educator. He spoke in both English and Spanish, making everyone feel comfortable.

He started with a simple truth: “Credit isn’t about being perfect. It’s about recovery.”

Lina felt seen.

Rafael explained the five components of a credit score : payment history (35%), utilization (30%), credit history length (15%), new credit (10%), and credit mix (10%). He emphasized that late payments were the most damaging, but also, the most fixable.

That night, Lina went home, opened her laptop, and pulled all three of her credit reports for free. The numbers were worse than she expected, late payments, a collection account, and high balances on all cards. But for the first time in a while, she felt ready to face it.

She made a list:

1. Pay off the smallest balance first – $312 on a store card.

2. Call all creditors to negotiate – especially the one in collections.

3. Set up automatic minimum payments – to avoid missing any more.

4. Create a budget – and stick to it, no matter how tight. She used her next weekend tips to pay off the store card entirely. Then she called the collection agency.

"I'd like to pay in full," she said. "But only if you'll agree to remove it from my credit report after payment."

To her surprise, they agreed. Two months later, the account disappeared from her report.

Her confidence grew.

She created an Excel tracker with due dates, balances, and interest rates. She highlighted every payment made and watched her progress over time.

One of the biggest lessons came from credit utilization . She had three cards, all over 85% usage. Rafael had said to aim for under 30%, and ideally under 10%. Lina called her longest-standing credit card company and requested a credit limit increase. She was approved, from $1,000 to $3,000, which instantly lowered her utilization percentage.

Then she set calendar reminders three days before each due date. No more late payments.

Six months into her recovery plan, her score climbed from 586 to 645.

It wasn't perfect, but it was progress.

She qualified for a lower-interest consolidation loan and used it to pay off two high-interest cards. Her monthly payments dropped by nearly $150, giving her breathing room in her budget.

That Christmas, she gifted herself peace of mind: no collection calls, no new missed payments, and, for the first time in two years, hope.

But Lina didn't stop with her own recovery.

She began sharing her story with other women in her community, stylists, nail techs, makeup artists, many of whom had also been hit hard by the pandemic. She held a "Credit & Coffee" meetup at her salon once a month, where they reviewed reports, disputed errors, and encouraged each other.

One stylist, Jessica, discovered a fraudulent account on her report. Lina helped her write the dispute letter. Another woman had a 580 score and didn't know she could rebuild it. Lina showed her how to get a secured card and use it smartly.

"Your credit doesn't define you," she told them. "But it can empower you."

By the end of the following year, Lina's score reached 703. She applied for a small business credit card again, not out of desperation, but as a tool. She used it for supplies and paid it off monthly, building both personal and business credit together.

She even financed a new salon chair, her first financed purchase in two years, and proudly paid it off early.

Looking back, Lina realized that her biggest mistake wasn't falling into debt.

It was ignoring it.

Once she faced her financial truth, the power came back into her hands. She didn't just rebuild her score, she rebuilt her identity as a confident, informed business owner.

And now, every time she sees a new stylist struggling with bills or avoiding credit entirely, she shares her story.

Because in Lina's eyes, knowledge isn't just power.

It's freedom.

CHAPTER 6: LONG-TERM CREDIT STRATEGIES

Now let's look at how to use your credit for long-term wealth building:

- Maintaining healthy credit habits for the long haul
- When and how to refinance for better terms
- Leveraging credit to build wealth through real estate and business
- Building a financial safety net to avoid dependency on credit
- Protecting your credit profile from identity theft and fraud

Let's start with maintaining good credit habits. Long-term credit success is built on consistency. Always pay your bills on time, keep your credit utilization low, and monitor your credit reports regularly. These habits not only help you maintain a strong score, but also signal to lenders that you're a responsible borrower. Next, consider refinancing opportunities. As your credit improves, you may qualify for lower interest rates on existing debts, like your mortgage, car loan, or student loans. Refinancing can save you thousands over time, but it's important to compare lenders, calculate total interest savings, and watch out for fees. Only refinance when the long-term savings outweigh the costs. Credit can also be a tool for wealth building. Once your credit is strong, you can leverage it to purchase appreciating assets, such as investment properties or business expansions. For example, using a mortgage to buy a rental property can generate cash flow and long-term equity. Similarly, using a business loan to grow your operations can increase income and asset value. The key is to borrow strategically and with a clear repayment plan. Another critical part of long-term success is building a financial safety net. This includes creating an emergency fund with at least 3–6 months of living expenses. A safety net helps you avoid going into debt when unexpected expenses arise, like car repairs or medical bills. It also gives you the flexibility to manage credit proactively instead of reactively. Finally, protect your credit profile. Identity theft and fraud can quickly damage years of careful credit building. Freeze your credit when not applying for new accounts, use strong passwords, and enable alerts for any suspicious activity. Check your credit reports regularly for unfamiliar accounts or inquiries, and act quickly if you suspect fraud. Long-term credit success doesn't require perfection, just consistency, awareness, and smart financial planning. Use these strategies not just to maintain your credit, but to turn it into a tool for true financial independence.

Luis Builds a Credit Legacy

Luis leaned back on his worn-out couch, watching a YouTube video titled, "How to Build Wealth in America." His 12-year-old son, Mateo, was doing homework at the kitchen table. The video host said something that stuck with Luis:

"Credit is more than a number. It's a tool. If you know how to use it, it can change your family's future."

That sentence echoed in Luis's mind. He hit pause and looked around his small apartment in Kissimmee, Florida. He and his wife, Carla, had immigrated from Honduras eight years earlier. Luis worked construction; Carla cleaned houses. They made just enough to cover bills, send money back home, and keep food on the table.

But Luis had dreams. Big and bold ones.

He wanted to buy a house. Start a business. Build something that would outlast him.

The problem? He didn't know where to start. He had never borrowed money. He paid for everything in cash and had no debt, but also no credit.

One day, while eating lunch on-site, Luis overheard a coworker talking about refinancing his house. "My credit score is up to 785," the guy bragged. Luis felt a pang of envy. That number, whatever it meant, seemed to open doors.

That night, Luis went online and searched, "How to get a credit score with no history." He stumbled across the idea of a secured credit card . He could pay a deposit, say $200, and use it just like a regular card. The bank would report his usage to the credit bureaus, and over time, he'd build a history.

He applied the next day.

Two weeks later, his card arrived. He felt nervous using it, but he committed to buying only gas and paying it off every Friday. "Slow and steady," he told himself.

Six months later, he had his first credit score: 662.

Encouraged, Luis took the next step. He visited a credit union and asked about a credit-builder loan . He didn't need to borrow money, but he understood now that this wasn't about cash, it was about proving consistency.

He took a $1,000 loan held in a savings account and paid $90 a month for 12 months. Each payment got reported to all three credit bureaus. He also became an authorized user on Carla's retail credit card, which had a five-year history.

Luis created a notebook where he wrote down due dates, balances, credit score updates, and even motivational quotes. Every time he paid early, he gave himself a gold star sticker, like a kid in school.

By the end of year one, Luis had a credit score of 710.

He was ready for his first big leap: buying a home.

He spoke to a mortgage broker, who walked him through the process. She recommended an FHA loan , which required a smaller down payment and accepted credit scores as low as 580, but Luis wanted the best rate possible.

He kept saving.

In six more months, he had $12,000, enough for a 3.5% down payment and closing costs. He was approved for a $250,000 FHA mortgage at 4.2%.

He and Carla found a three-bedroom home in a quiet neighborhood near Mateo's school. They were outbid on the first offer, but the second one stuck.

Luis had never signed so many papers in his life. But as the mortgage agent handed him the keys, he felt something deeper than excitement.

He felt power.

Two years after buying their home, Luis refinanced the loan at 3.3% as his credit score climbed to 765. He used the monthly savings to start investing in tools and gear for a side hustle, installing fences and patios on weekends. With consistent income and a strong credit profile, he opened his first business credit card under an LLC. He used it only for business expenses and paid it in full each month. It helped him separate personal and business finances, and slowly build business credit too.

By his fourth year in the U.S. credit system, Luis owned a home, operated a side business, and had three credit cards, all paid in full. His credit report had zero missed payments.

But Luis wasn't finished.

One Saturday, Mateo came into the kitchen holding a college brochure.

"Dad, will my student loans mess up my credit?"

Luis smiled. "Not if you learn now what I had to learn the hard way."

He sat Mateo down and explained what a credit score was, how to check it, and how to start small. They opened a student credit card together, with a $300 limit, and Luis co-signed. He taught Mateo the same golden rules: keep your balance under 10%, pay early, never miss a bill.

Together, they made the first payment.

It was a proud moment, not because of the dollar amount, but because of what it represented.

Legacy.

Luis began volunteering at a local community center teaching "Credit 101" to other immigrants. He shared his journey, his systems, and his mistakes. He told them not to be afraid of credit, just to respect it.

He taught families how to read credit reports, dispute errors, and build a plan. He translated letters into Spanish, called customer service on behalf of nervous parents, and even helped one woman negotiate a collection account down from $1,400 to $580.

"You don't need to be rich to build credit," he told them. "You just need to be consistent."

Luis's story became a beacon for many who thought credit was out of reach. He showed that with patience, knowledge, and community, even someone starting from zero could rise above.

Today, Luis's credit score holds steady above 770. He owns a duplex and is looking for a third rental property. Mateo is in his second year of college and has a score of 712. Carla runs her own cleaning business and just got approved for a $10,000 business line of credit.

The best part? Luis never became a slave to credit.

He used it intentionally, carefully, and with the bigger picture in mind.

He didn't just build a score.

He built a future.

And that future would outlive him.

CHAPTER 7: TURNING CREDIT INTO CAPITAL, THE POWER OF FINANCIAL LEVERAGE

Most people think of credit as just a number, a score that gets you a loan, a car, or a credit card. But what if I told you that credit can be much more than that? What if, instead of just borrowing for purchases, you learned how to use credit to create income, wealth, and freedom?

In this final chapter, we'll explore a topic that goes beyond the basics, how to leverage your credit into capital, and turn that capital into long-term opportunity. This is where credit stops being just a tool to buy things and starts becoming a gateway to building wealth, investing in yourself, and funding your dreams.

Let's get creative.

Credit as Leverage – Not Just a Score

Once you've established good credit, meaning a score in the mid-700s or higher, low utilization, and a strong payment history, you have something incredibly valuable: trust in the eyes of lenders.

That trust can be converted into capital, real, usable money in the form of:

- Business credit cards
- Personal lines of credit
- Installment loans
- Home equity loans
- 0% APR intro offers
- And in some cases, even grants or SBA-backed loans

The power of that capital depends on how you use it. Many people waste their borrowing ability on short-term gratification, TVs, vacations, impulse spending. But the most successful individuals use their credit to create cash-generating opportunities.

Smart Ways to Turn Credit Into Income

Here are a few strategic examples of how people have turned good credit into opportunity:

1. Starting a Small Business

Once you have strong personal credit, you can access 0% APR business credit cards or lines of credit. Many entrepreneurs have launched online stores, tutoring services, or freelance businesses using just a few thousand dollars in startup funds, all funded by their credit.

Example: Angela, a recent immigrant from Brazil, used her 750 credit score to open two business cards with 12 months at 0% interest. She bought inventory, created a Shopify store, and reinvested profits. Within six months, she was making $2,000/month in profit, with no interest paid.

2. Real Estate Investing

With good credit, you can qualify for low-down-payment FHA loans, or even home equity lines of credit (HELOCs) if you already own property. Some investors even use 0% APR cards to fund renovations, flip properties, or furnish rentals.

Example: Jamal used his credit score of 780 to buy a duplex with 3.5% down. He lived in one side and rented out the other. His tenant covered 80% of his mortgage, giving him cash flow and appreciation.

3. Credit Arbitrage

Though risky if misused, credit arbitrage involves borrowing at 0% APR and investing in assets that yield more than the cost of borrowing. Some do this with high-yield savings, inventory for resale, or even purchasing equipment for a side hustle.

Warning: Only attempt this with a solid plan and the ability to pay back before interest kicks in.

Building a Funding Plan Using Your Credit

If you're ready to take your credit beyond consumer spending, here's a step-by-step framework to responsibly leverage it for growth:

Step 1: Know Your Limits

Request credit limit increases on your existing accounts (without hard pulls where possible). This increases your available credit, reduces utilization, and gives you more flexibility.

Step 2: Create a Business Idea or Investment Goal

What would you do if you had access to $5,000 tomorrow? Fund a course and start freelancing? Build a digital product? Buy equipment for your cleaning business? Clarity is power.

Step 3: Apply for Strategic Credit

Research business credit cards with long 0% APR offers, or apply for a personal line of credit with your bank. Don't use this credit for consumption, only creation.

Step 4: Use Capital for Asset-Building

Spend only on things that can return income: marketing, inventory, equipment, training, or systems. Avoid depreciating items or personal luxuries.

Step 5: Track ROI and Set Payback Timelines

Always set a deadline to repay the borrowed capital, even before the 0% interest period ends. If your project fails to create income, stop spending and pay off what you owe.

The Credit-Opportunity Flywheel

As you start to successfully use credit to fund profitable projects, something powerful happens: your credit improves further, your income grows, and you gain access to even more capital. This creates what we call a credit-opportunity flywheel:

You build credit.

You use it to create something valuable.

You repay on time and profit from your project.

Your credit improves again.

Lenders offer even better terms.

You scale your opportunities.

It's a cycle that can take someone from $0 to a thriving business, portfolio, or even early retirement.

And it starts with responsible credit habits.

A Legacy Mindset

Luis, from Chapter 6, didn't just use credit to buy a house. He used it to start a family business, mentor his son, and teach his community. That's credit with purpose.

You can do the same.

Start thinking beyond survival and toward legacy. What can you build today with your current credit profile? How can your story inspire someone else?

Ask yourself:

- Can I launch a service business?
- Can I publish a book or course?
- Can I rent a property and build equity?
- Can I invest in education that pays off?

If the answer is yes, you have everything you need.

Final Thoughts

Credit is not just a score. It's not just a loan. It's not just a card.

Credit is permission to create.

You've learned how to establish credit, improve it, and now, how to turn it into something greater. This is your invitation to think big, act smart, and use your credit to not just finance things... but to finance a life of possibility.

The world doesn't just need consumers. It needs creators. Builders. Leaders.

Your credit can help you become one.

So go out there. Dream boldly. Plan wisely. And remember: you're not just building credit, you're building a life that lasts.

Elena's Leap from Credit Score to Capital

Elena sat at the edge of her bed, staring at the balance in her bank account: $672.14. She had enough to cover groceries, her phone bill, and maybe gas for the week, but there was nothing left for dreams. She sighed and refreshed the screen again, as if willing the number to rise.

It wasn't that Elena was careless with money. Quite the opposite. Since moving from Guatemala to Phoenix five years earlier, she had lived frugally, worked full-time as a medical assistant, and slowly built a life she could call her own. But despite her efforts, she felt stuck, renting a small apartment, working extra shifts, and wondering if she'd ever be able to afford anything bigger.

Then one night, while scrolling TikTok, she came across a video that changed her trajectory.

The creator said, "If you have a good credit score, you're sitting on opportunity. Not debt. Not limits. Leverage."

That word hit Elena like lightning: leverage.

She clicked the profile, then the link to a free credit-building workshop. It was the first time she'd heard someone explain that credit wasn't just for buying, it could be used to build. Build businesses. Build assets. Build income.

Elena had spent the last three years improving her credit. She had started with a secured credit card, paid every bill on time, kept her balances low, and now had a FICO score of 741. But she hadn't done anything with it, she was afraid of going backward.

The workshop host said something she couldn't forget: "If your credit is strong and your mindset is smart, you're in a better position than most. The next step is to turn that score into capital, and that capital into something valuable."

Elena stayed up all night researching business ideas. She had always loved baking and decorating cakes. She even had a side hustle selling tres leches and cupcakes to coworkers and friends. Could she turn that into something more?

She wrote a list of everything she'd need:

- A commercial mixer
- Packaging supplies
- A small website
- Licensing and permits
- A second refrigerator for ingredients

The total came to just under $3,000.

Elena didn't have that in savings, but her credit offered a path forward.

The next week, she applied for a business credit card with 12 months at 0% APR. She was approved for $4,000. For the first time, credit didn't feel like a trap, it felt like a tool.

Elena used it wisely. She purchased only what she needed to scale. She built a simple website using a free template. She took orders online and arranged weekend pickups from her apartment kitchen.

Within two months, her weekend baking income surpassed her weekday job.

But Elena didn't stop there.

She applied for a business license, joined a local women's entrepreneur group, and took a free class on bookkeeping and taxes. She made a repayment plan and set auto-payments on her credit card to eliminate the debt before interest kicked in.

By month nine, her card was paid off.

Her credit score? Still above 740.

Her new problem? Too many customers.

That fall, she applied for a small business line of credit, $15,000, this time backed by a combination of personal credit and new business revenue. She used it to put a deposit on a shared commercial kitchen space and hired her cousin part-time.

What started with a credit card had turned into a full-fledged baking business.

By year two, Elena was earning $6,500 a month in revenue and had opened a storefront. She named it Cielo Dulce, Sweet Heaven.

But what made Elena the proudest wasn't the money.

It was freedom.

She was able to reduce her hours at her day job and spend more time with her daughter. She helped her mom get approved for her first credit card. She hosted a workshop at her local library on how to build credit and fund side hustles.

And one Saturday morning, when her daughter asked how she started her bakery, Elena didn't hesitate.

"I started with good credit," she said. "But more importantly, I believed I could use it to build something."

Elena's story proves that credit is not the destination, it's the bridge. The question isn't whether you should use credit, but whether you'll use it wisely, with purpose and a plan.

She used hers to build a business. Others use it to invest, to scale, to create.

Because when credit meets clarity and courage?

Anything is possible.

CONCLUSION

Congratulations on completing How to Establish Credit in the U.S.: Unlock Financial Freedom as an Immigrant!

You've taken a major step toward mastering one of the most powerful tools for financial stability and growth: your credit. Whether you were starting from zero, repairing past mistakes, or looking to move your credit to the next level, this book has given you the roadmap to do just that.

Let's take a moment to reflect on what you've accomplished:

- You've gained a clear understanding of how the U.S. credit system works, including credit scores, reports, and the roles of the three major credit bureaus.

- You learned how to start building credit from scratch with proven methods like secured credit cards, credit-builder loans, and authorized user status.

- You explored how to improve your credit score through practical actions like lowering your utilization, disputing errors, and building consistent habits.

- You discovered how to strategically finance major purchases, like cars, homes, and businesses, using credit wisely and responsibly.

- You identified the most common credit mistakes and learned how to avoid them so your progress stays on track.

- And you finished by developing a long-term strategy for using credit as a tool to build wealth, protect your financial future, and unlock greater freedom. But your journey doesn't end here. Credit is a living, evolving part of your financial life. It requires ongoing attention and care. As you continue down your path, keep reviewing your goals.

Ask yourself: Where do I want to be financially in 1 year?

3 years?

10 years?

Your credit profile can and should help you get there. Here are a few next steps to take immediately:

1. Pull your free credit report from AnnualCreditReport.com and review it carefully.

2. Apply one improvement strategy today. Whether it's paying off a balance, setting up auto-pay, or becoming an authorized user, take action.

3. Set a reminder to review your credit score monthly and track your progress.

4. Share what you've learned. If this book helped you, consider sharing it with a friend, family member, or coworker who could benefit.

As we conclude, I want to remind you that your past does not define your financial future. No matter where you're starting from, you have the power to change your credit story and create a life filled with options, freedom, and peace of mind. Credit is more than a score, it's a gateway to stability, security, and success.

I also want to thank you sincerely for spending this time with me. I created this book because I've seen firsthand how difficult it can be to navigate the U.S. credit system as an immigrant or first-time user. My goal was to simplify it, empower you, and give you a clear action plan, and I hope I've done that for you. If you found this book valuable, I would greatly appreciate it if you could leave a review. Your feedback helps others discover this guide and supports me in continuing to create tools that help people like you succeed.

To stay connected and get access to more tools, downloads, and financial education resources or to simply contact me for financing, visit finibimortgage.com or follow me on social media at @finibimortgage.

Thank you again, and remember: Your credit is not just about numbers. It's about access. It's about opportunity. It's about your future. Keep moving forward. Stay consistent. And I'll see you on your journey to financial freedom.

All the best,

Joe Correa

Author, educator, and advocate for financial empowerment.

Other Books in the *Credit to Capital* Series

By Joe Correa

Unlock the full financial journey with these powerful and practical audiobooks in the *Credit to Capital* series. Each volume is designed to help you build, repair, and leverage credit to create wealth, purchase property, and launch businesses—no matter where you're starting from.

- **Book 1: How to Establish Credit in the U.S.**
- **Book 2: Personal Credit Repair Blueprint**
- **Book 3: How to Build Credit Fast Without Debt**
- **Book 4: Business Credit Mastery**
- **Book 5: Credit Card Secrets for Building Wealth & Rewards**
- **Book 6: Credit Card Hacking for Smart Borrowers**
- **Book 7: How to Leverage Business Credit to Fund Real Estate Purchases**
- **Book 8: Business Credit Ecosystem: Build, Stack & Automate Unlimited Funding Without Personal Risk**
- **Book 9: How to Get $1M in Credit and Keep It**
- **Book 10: Credit-Funded Wealth for Families**

www.ingramcontent.com/pod-product-compliance
Lightning Source LLC
LaVergne TN
LVHW020236210926
848481LV00016B/2341
* 9 7 9 8 8 6 9 1 3 5 6 1 2 *